Pebble® Plus

A Butterfly's
Life Cycle

Mary R Du

raintree
a Capstone company — publishers for children

Raintree is an imprint of Capstone Global Library Limited, a company incorporated in England and Wales having its registered office at 264 Banbury Road, Oxford, OX2 7DY – Registered company number: 6695582

www.raintree.co.uk
myorders@raintree.co.uk

Edited by Anna Butzer
Designed by Kyle Grenz
Picture research by Wanda Winch
Production by Kathy McColley
Originated by Capstone Global Library Ltd
Printed and bound in China

ISBN 978 1 4747 4330 3
21 20 19 18 17
10 9 8 7 6 5 4 3 2 1

British Library Cataloguing in Publication Data
A full catalogue record for this book is available from the British Library.

Acknowledgements
We would like to thank the following for permission to reproduce photographs: Dreamstime: Rinusbaak, back cover, 19; Shutterstock: Sari ONeal, 17, Cathy Keifer, 7, D. Longenbaugh, cover, del Monaco, 15, jaimie Tuchman, 9, Kim Howell, 21, Leena Robinson, 11, 13, Mike Vande Ven Jr., 1, nemlaza, butterfly silhouettes, Perry Correll, 5

Every effort has been made to contact copyright holders of material reproduced in this book. Any omissions will be rectified in subsequent printings if notice is given to the publisher.

All the internet addresses (URLs) given in this book were valid at the time of going to press. However, due to the dynamic nature of the internet, some addresses may have changed, or sites may have changed or ceased to exist since publication. While the author and publisher regret any inconvenience this may cause readers, no responsibility for any such changes can be accepted by either the author or the publisher.

Contents

Life in an egg

A female monarch butterfly floats in
the air. She is looking for a special plant.
At last she finds a milkweed plant
and lays her eggs.

Caterpillars hatch from the eggs in about a week. They eat their way out of the egg using their strong jaws.

Hungry caterpillars

Hungry caterpillars eat milkweed leaves.

They eat until their skin gets too tight. Pop!

They moult, or shed their old skins.

Underneath is a new, larger skin.

9

A caterpillar sheds its skin four or

five times. The caterpillar hangs

upside down from a leaf.

It sheds its skin one more time.

The new layer is called a pupa or chrysalis.

11

Inside a pupa

The pupa hardens as it dries.
Inside the pupa, a caterpillar's
body changes. After about
two weeks, the pupa cracks open.

13

A butterfly pulls itself out of the pupa.
Its body is wet and folded. Its wings
slowly open and dry in the sun.

15

Life as a butterfly

All summer the monarch flies

from flower to flower.

It unrolls its long tongue to eat.

The monarch sucks nectar

from the flowers. Yum!

Days get shorter. The weather
gets cooler. Monarch butterflies know
it is time for the long flight south.
They rest in trees along the way.

In spring, the sun warms the butterflies. Most fly north. Butterflies mate and the females lay eggs. Caterpillars hatch and moult. And from a pupa comes a beautiful butterfly!

GLOSSARY

caterpillar larva that changes into a butterfly or moth; a caterpillar is the second life stage of a butterfly

chrysalis hard shell inside which a pupa changes into a butterfly

hatch break out of an egg

jaw part of the mouth used to grab, bite and chew

mate join together to produce young; a mate is also the male or female partner of a pair of animals

milkweed plant with milky juice and pointed pods; monarch butterflies lay eggs only on milkweed

moult shed an outer layer of skin

nectar sweet liquid found in many flowers

pupa hard casing with an animal inside; the animal is changing from larval stage to the final animal stage

FIND OUT MORE

BOOKS

Lifecycles (Ways into Science), Peter Riley (Franklin Watts, 2016)

Life Story of a Butterfly (Animal Life Stories), Charlotte Guillain (Heinemann Library, 2014)

The Incredible Life Cycle of a Butterfly, Kay Barnham (Wayland, 2017)

WEBSITES

www.bbc.co.uk/education/clips/zfqd7ty
This video shows all the life stages of a butterfly.

www.ngkids.co.uk/science-and-nature/butterfly-life-cycle
Follow the life cycles of a butterfly and a moth on this website.

COMPREHENSION QUESTIONS

1. What are the stages of a butterfly's life?

2. A caterpillar moults. How many times does it moult before it is fully grown?

3. In the glossary, find the word that tells what caterpillars eat.

INDEX